MW01171719

# Release
# The FOG
# (Favor Of God)

# Journal

Unless otherwise indicated all Scriptures are taken from the NJKV.
*Release The FOG Journal*
ISBN-10:0615739067
Copyright @2012
All publishing rights belong exclusively to Jerry Grillo Ministries.
P.O. Box 3707 Hickory, NC. 28603
1-888-367-5383 www.bishopgrillo.com
Printed in the United States of America. All rights reserved under International Copyright laws.
Content and/or cover may not be reproduced in whole or in part in any form without the
express written consent of the publisher.

| TOPIC | THOUGHT |
|---|---|

_____
_____
_____
_____
_____
_____
_____
_____
_____
_____
_____
_____
_____
_____
_____
_____
_____
_____
_____
_____
_____
_____
_____
_____
_____
_____
_____

*"The unholy are always unthankful! Favor always follows a life that is thankful! Be thankful every day, not just one day..." Dr. G*

| TOPIC | THOUGHT |
|---|---|

| TOPIC | THOUGHT |
|-------|---------|

_____

_____

_____

_____

_____

_____

_____

_____

_____

_____

_____

_____

_____

_____

_____

_____

_____

_____

_____

_____

_____

_____

_____

_____

*"Jesus tolerated ignorance, worked on preaching them truth. He never accepted their ignorance & allowed it to be okay! We must keep truth! " Dr. G*

| TOPIC | THOUGHT |
|-------|---------|

_____
_____
_____
_____
_____
_____
_____
_____
_____
_____
_____
_____
_____
_____
_____
_____
_____
_____
_____
_____
_____
_____
_____
_____
_____

*"God Favored Mary because He knew He could trust her reaction when people would criticize her condition. Reaction reveals you!" Dr. G*

TOPIC | THOUGHT

| TOPIC | THOUGHT |
|-------|---------|

_"Amateurs built the Ark with God's help and survived a destroying catastrophe. Professionals built the Titanic using man's wisdom and an iceberg sank it."_ Dr. G

| TOPIC | THOUGHT |
| --- | --- |
| | |

| TOPIC | THOUGHT |
|-------|---------|
|       |         |

_"What you keep is your harvest. What you sow is your seed."_ Dr. G

| TOPIC | THOUGHT |
|-------|---------|

| TOPIC | THOUGHT |
|-------|---------|

_____
_____
_____
_____
_____
_____
_____
_____
_____
_____
_____
_____
_____
_____
_____
_____
_____
_____
_____
_____
_____
_____
_____
_____

*"My offering to God is my conversation to God that there is something I am believing Him for and am persuaded that He's the source that will provide."*
*Dr. G*

# TOPIC | THOUGHT

# TOPIC | THOUGHT

_____
_____
_____
_____
_____
_____
_____
_____
_____
_____
_____
_____
_____
_____
_____
_____
_____
_____
_____
_____
_____
_____
_____
_____
_____
_____

*"No matter what life has sent your way, don't let your dream die away. Keep it guarded... Keep it hidden deep within you. It will happen!" Dr. G*

| TOPIC | THOUGHT |
|---|---|

| TOPIC | THOUGHT |
| --- | --- |

_____
_____
_____
_____
_____
_____
_____
_____
_____
_____
_____
_____
_____
_____
_____
_____
_____
_____
_____
_____
_____
_____

*"Never make money your priority! Money is simply a moment's reward for a moment of work! Find your divine purpose. God will send His FAVOR. A season of reward is scheduled!" Dr. G*

| TOPIC | THOUGHT |
| --- | --- |

| TOPIC | THOUGHT |
| --- | --- |

_"Seek God's Majesty more than you seek God's Miracles. God is epic! God is Awesome! God is worthy of your focus and your praise!" Dr. G_

TOPIC | THOUGHT

| TOPIC | THOUGHT |
|---|---|

_"Money doesn't produce purpose... it pays for it! Never make money your focus. Find your purpose and money will find you."_ Dr. G

| TOPIC | THOUGHT |
|-------|---------|

_____
_____
_____
_____
_____
_____
_____
_____
_____
_____
_____
_____
_____
_____
_____
_____
_____
_____
_____
_____
_____
_____
_____
_____
_____
_____
_____
_____

*"God's kingdom is a sure investment, a guaranteed return. People would rather gamble in the world than release their seeds in the Kingdom! Harvest is always the result for sowing." Dr. G*

TOPIC | THOUGHT

| TOPIC | THOUGHT |
|-------|---------|

_____

_____

_____

_____

_____

_____

_____

_____

_____

_____

_____

_____

_____

_____

_____

_____

_____

_____

_____

_____

_____

_____

_____

_____

_____

*"The danger of money is that it can have you become more focused on things and not purpose. Money doesn't produce purpose; it pays for it!" Dr. G*

TOPIC | THOUGHT

# TOPIC | THOUGHT

_____
_____
_____
_____
_____
_____
_____
_____
_____
_____
_____
_____
_____
_____
_____
_____
_____
_____
_____
_____
_____
_____
_____
_____

*"Don't lose focus in times of financial comfort. You must keep growing your business. Remember nothing is permanent!" Dr. G*

| TOPIC | THOUGHT |
|-------|---------|
|       |         |

| TOPIC | THOUGHT |
|-------|---------|

_"I don't know what you're facing today. If you are in the kingdom of God then remember, God has the last word. So work on keeping your faith intact!" Dr. G_

| TOPIC | THOUGHT |
|-------|---------|

_____
_____
_____
_____
_____
_____
_____
_____
_____
_____
_____
_____
_____
_____
_____
_____
_____
_____
_____
_____
_____
_____
_____
_____
_____
_____
_____
_____

*"Unforgiveness, bitterness, and dissension are cancers to the spirit man! Release them today. Nothing should have that kind of power over you."* Dr. G

| TOPIC | THOUGHT |
|-------|---------|

_____
_____
_____
_____
_____
_____
_____
_____
_____
_____
_____
_____
_____
_____
_____
_____
_____
_____
_____
_____
_____
_____
_____
_____
_____
_____

*"Christianity isn't a part-time position. It is full-time living. Christianity is not what we do; it's who we ARE! Don't forget it!" Dr. G*

TOPIC | THOUGHT

| TOPIC | THOUGHT |
|---|---|

_"Confession without change is nothing but an attempt to stop the guilt of the infraction without the heart being convinced by conviction."_ Dr. G

TOPIC | THOUGHT

_____

_____

_____

_____

_____

_____

_____

_____

_____

_____

_____

_____

_____

_____

_____

_____

_____

_____

_____

_____

_____

_____

_____

_____

_____

_____

_____

*"Incentive; everything on the earth works around incentive. Jesus always gave us an incentive for our actions! Give, I'll give back more. Confess Me; I'll give you life!" Dr. G*

| TOPIC | THOUGHT |
|---|---|
|  |  |

| TOPIC | THOUGHT |
|-------|---------|

*"Bitterness is the poison swallowed waiting for the other person to suffer for hurting you! It's the cancer of the soul and keeps you from healing!" Dr. G*

TOPIC | THOUGHT

| TOPIC | THOUGHT |
|---|---|

*"Beware of people that want **AUTHORITY** without **ACCOUNTABILITY**."*
*Dr. G*

| TOPIC | THOUGHT |
|-------|---------|

| TOPIC | THOUGHT |
|---|---|

*"When you've moved from prosperity to famine, there's a reason."* Dr. G

TOPIC | THOUGHT

| TOPIC | THOUGHT |
|-------|---------|

_____
_____
_____
_____
_____
_____
_____
_____
_____
_____
_____
_____
_____
_____
_____
_____
_____
_____
_____
_____
_____
_____
_____
_____
_____

*"Adam didn't know he had Eve in him until God pulled her out. We must trust God. He knows what he has locked up inside of us; Destiny and Future!"*
*Dr. G*

| TOPIC | THOUGHT |
| --- | --- |

_"The difference between Faith and Fear: Fear creates worry; Faith creates worship! Fear paralyzes your hopes; Faith ignites your hopes! God is moved by your faith." Dr. G_

| TOPIC | THOUGHT |
|-------|---------|

_"You can't have faith and reason in the same room! At times, faith just makes no sense at all!" Dr. G_

| TOPIC | THOUGHT |
|-------|---------|
|       |         |

| TOPIC | THOUGHT |
|-------|---------|

_"Winners are not those who never fail but those who NEVER QUIT! Endurance is the proof you have a winner inside of you. Keep Trying!"_ Dr. G

| TOPIC | THOUGHT |
|---|---|

_"Thankfulness is a powerful atmosphere changer. It will always replenish the atmosphere for miracles to happen. Be grateful everyday!" Dr. G_

| TOPIC | THOUGHT |
|-------|---------|
|       |         |

| TOPIC | THOUGHT |
|-------|---------|

_____
_____
_____
_____
_____
_____
_____
_____
_____
_____
_____
_____
_____
_____
_____
_____
_____
_____
_____
_____
_____
_____
_____
_____
_____
_____

*"When you break a law, you create a loss. When you obey a law, you create a reward." Dr. G*

| TOPIC | THOUGHT |
|-------|---------|
|       |         |

_"Waiting is the proof you have a secure mind and a solid trust in God's ability to lead you. Hurrying always misses the best blessings. **Waiters are winners!**"Dr. G_

TOPIC | THOUGHT

| TOPIC | THOUGHT |
|---|---|

_"Failure can become the womb for success. Failure may be the only way God can wake up the Eve inside you. You're being prepared to produce more!"_
_Dr. G_

| TOPIC | THOUGHT |
|-------|---------|
|       |         |

TOPIC | THOUGHT

_"Stop waiting on someone to come & rescue you! Noah didn't wait for his ship to come in. Noah built his ship! Start doing something now to succeed." Dr. G_

| TOPIC | THOUGHT |
|-------|---------|
|       |         |

| TOPIC | THOUGHT |
|---|---|

_"Government leaders are elected. Kingdom leaders are selected; they are chosen! Government leaders last 8 years. Selected leaders last until God comes!" Dr. G_

| TOPIC | THOUGHT |
|-------|---------|
|       |         |

| TOPIC | THOUGHT |
|-------|---------|

_____
_____
_____
_____
_____
_____
_____
_____
_____
_____
_____
_____
_____
_____
_____
_____
_____
_____
_____
_____
_____
_____
_____
_____
_____

*"It was never God's "will" or plan for people to live on a fixed income. He planned on us living on our GIVING!" Dr. G*

| TOPIC | THOUGHT |
| --- | --- |

| TOPIC | THOUGHT |
|-------|---------|

_____
_____
_____
_____
_____
_____
_____
_____
_____
_____
_____
_____
_____
_____
_____
_____
_____
_____
_____
_____
_____
_____
_____
_____
_____

*"Don't like your living? Then change your giving. If you hate what has grown in the garden of your mind, then change what seeds you have sown into it."*
*Dr. G*

| TOPIC | THOUGHT |
|---|---|

_____
_____
_____
_____
_____
_____
_____
_____
_____
_____
_____
_____
_____
_____
_____
_____
_____
_____
_____
_____
_____
_____
_____
_____

*"Money isn't the root of all evil. What people do with money is what makes it evil."*
*Dr. G*

| TOPIC | THOUGHT |
| --- | --- |

_"You will never be in Authority if you are not under Authority!" Dr. G_

| TOPIC | THOUGHT |
|---|---|

TOPIC | THOUGHT

_____
_____
_____
_____
_____
_____
_____
_____
_____
_____
_____
_____
_____
_____
_____
_____
_____
_____
_____
_____
_____
_____
_____
_____
_____
_____
_____
_____
_____
_____

*"Never allow the loss of money to rob you of the power of faith. Money is a reward for work...Faith is a belief in something bigger! Jesus!" Dr. G*

TOPIC | THOUGHT

| TOPIC | THOUGHT |
|-------|---------|

_"You may have to give up your stuff in times of crisis; but never give up your faith! One season of Favor can replenish everything you've lost!" Dr. G_

| TOPIC | THOUGHT |
|-------|---------|
|       |         |

| TOPIC | THOUGHT |
|---|---|

_____
_____
_____
_____
_____
_____
_____
_____
_____
_____
_____
_____
_____
_____
_____
_____
_____
_____
_____
_____
_____
_____
_____
_____
_____
_____
_____

*"When you lose your fight, you've lost your hope for tomorrow. Defeat is now settling in your mind. Defeat robs you of your creative thinking." Dr. G*

TOPIC | THOUGHT

## TOPIC | THOUGHT

_"Discouragement means you've now become enslaved to your circumstances. You are now talking more about your pain, than your way out! Stay encouraged!" Dr. G_

TOPIC | THOUGHT

| TOPIC | THOUGHT |
|-------|---------|

_____
_____
_____
_____
_____
_____
_____
_____
_____
_____
_____
_____
_____
_____
_____
_____
_____
_____
_____
_____
_____
_____
_____
_____
_____
_____
_____
_____

*"The difference between those who endure with faith and those who are just enduring is expectation! Faith keeps your expectation alive for restoration."*
*Dr. G*

| TOPIC | THOUGHT |
|-------|---------|

| TOPIC | THOUGHT |
|-------|---------|

_"Remember to celebrate the harvest more than the seed! You are about to REAP!" Dr. G_

| TOPIC | THOUGHT |
|-------|---------|

| TOPIC | THOUGHT |
|---|---|

_"The difference in seasons is simple information. Something you don't know is keeping you imprisoned to what you already know." Dr. G_

| TOPIC | THOUGHT |
|---|---|

| TOPIC | THOUGHT |
|-------|---------|

*"Money can buy you a house, but it can't buy you a home. Money can buy you things, but it can't buy you peace of mind." Dr. G*

| TOPIC | THOUGHT |
|-------|---------|
|       |         |

| TOPIC | THOUGHT |
|-------|---------|

_"Those who do not discern your worth disqualify for your friendship."_ Dr. G

| TOPIC | THOUGHT |
|-------|---------|

| TOPIC | THOUGHT |
|-------|---------|

_____

_____

_____

_____

_____

_____

_____

_____

_____

_____

_____

_____

_____

_____

_____

_____

_____

_____

_____

_____

_____

_____

_____

_____

_____

_____

*"Anything you're becoming is the result of pressure. Under pressure you will either focus or fold." Dr. G*

| TOPIC | THOUGHT |
|-------|---------|

| TOPIC | THOUGHT |
|-------|---------|

_"There's a difference between involvement and commitment. The proof is your loyalty during a crisis. Lot was involved but Abraham was committed!" Dr. G_

TOPIC | THOUGHT

*"Our flaws cause us to work that much harder to find God and His perfect ways. Flaws are the keys that unlock our pursuit for change."* Dr. G

TOPIC | THOUGHT

## TOPIC | THOUGHT

_____
_____
_____
_____
_____
_____
_____
_____
_____
_____
_____
_____
_____
_____
_____
_____
_____
_____
_____
_____
_____
_____
_____
_____
_____
_____
_____
_____
_____

_"When you find wisdom, you have found the Lord and you will obtain Favor!_
_That favor is debt cancellation. I speak debts to be removed today."_
_Proverbs 8:35_

TOPIC | THOUGHT

| TOPIC | THOUGHT |
|---|---|

_"Relationships work best when you're committed to the relationship and not just involved in it! Being for someone is greater than just doing for them!"_
_Dr. G_

| TOPIC | THOUGHT |
|-------|---------|

| TOPIC | THOUGHT |
|-------|---------|

_____
_____
_____
_____
_____
_____
_____
_____
_____
_____
_____
_____
_____
_____
_____
_____
_____
_____
_____
_____
_____
_____
_____
_____
_____
_____
_____
_____
_____
_____

*"Knowledge is found in books. Knowledge understands the ways of man. Wisdom is when you discern the ways of God." Dr. G*

| TOPIC | THOUGHT |
|---|---|

| TOPIC | THOUGHT |
|-------|---------|

_____
_____
_____
_____
_____
_____
_____
_____
_____
_____
_____
_____
_____
_____
_____
_____
_____
_____
_____
_____
_____
_____
_____
_____
_____
_____

*"Wrong people can stop God's promotion in your life! Wrong people can slow down your harvest!" Dr. G*

TOPIC | THOUGHT

| TOPIC | THOUGHT |
|-------|---------|

_____
_____
_____
_____
_____
_____
_____
_____
_____
_____
_____
_____
_____
_____
_____
_____
_____
_____
_____
_____
_____
_____
_____
_____
_____
_____

*"When God has decided to favor your life, hell has decided to oppose your favor. Expect warfare to surround a favored life." Dr. G*

| TOPIC | THOUGHT |
|-------|---------|
|       |         |

*"Favor is a seed before it is a Harvest."* Dr. G

| TOPIC | THOUGHT |
|-------|---------|

*"Expect a season of reward on the other side of obedience."* Dr. G

TOPIC | THOUGHT

| TOPIC | THOUGHT |
|-------|---------|

_____
_____
_____
_____
_____
_____
_____
_____
_____
_____
_____
_____
_____
_____
_____
_____
_____
_____
_____
_____
_____
_____
_____
_____
_____
_____
_____
_____
_____
_____

*"Obedience schedules seasons of rewards… disobeying God's laws always schedules seasons of loss." Dr. G*

| TOPIC | THOUGHT |
|-------|---------|

_"Prosperity is a choice... Prosperity is granted by reward... Prosperity is the fruit of favor."_ Dr. G

| TOPIC | THOUGHT |
|-------|---------|

| TOPIC | THOUGHT |
|-------|---------|

_"Invest what is necessary to create the proper atmosphere that will keep you inspired."_ Dr. G

| TOPIC | THOUGHT |
|-------|---------|
|       |         |

| TOPIC | THOUGHT |
|-------|---------|

_____
_____
_____
_____
_____
_____
_____
_____
_____
_____
_____
_____
_____
_____
_____
_____
_____
_____
_____
_____
_____
_____
_____
_____
_____
_____
_____

*"Reaction is bigger than your praise… Reaction reveals you… In times of crisis monitor your reaction."* Dr. G

| TOPIC | THOUGHT |
|-------|---------|
|       |         |

| TOPIC | THOUGHT |
|---|---|

_"Reaction decides your access. Reaction decides who gets close to you."_ Dr. G

TOPIC | THOUGHT

| TOPIC | THOUGHT |
|---|---|

_____
_____
_____
_____
_____
_____
_____
_____
_____
_____
_____
_____
_____
_____
_____
_____
_____
_____
_____
_____
_____
_____
_____
_____
_____
_____

*"If your boss is dreading your entry, they have already decided your exit."*
*Dr. G*

# TOPIC

# THOUGHT

| TOPIC | THOUGHT |
|-------|---------|
|       |         |

*"Pride will always produce the wrong reaction."* Dr. G

| TOPIC | THOUGHT |
|-------|---------|
|       |         |

_"Reaction decides the longevity of an offense."_ Dr. G

| TOPIC | THOUGHT |
|-------|---------|
|       |         |

| TOPIC | THOUGHT |
|-------|---------|

*"There is no fruit that is not bitter before it is ripe."* Dr. G

TOPIC | THOUGHT

_____

_____

_____

_____

_____

_____

_____

_____

_____

_____

_____

_____

_____

_____

_____

_____

_____

_____

_____

_____

_____

_____

_____

_____

_____

_____

_____

_____

_____

*"Fear is hell's currency for stopping miracles. Faith is God's currency to release miracles." Dr. G*

TOPIC | THOUGHT

| TOPIC | THOUGHT |
|-------|---------|

_____

_____

_____

_____

_____

_____

_____

_____

_____

_____

_____

_____

_____

_____

_____

_____

_____

_____

_____

_____

_____

_____

_____

_____

_____

_____

_____

_____

_____

*"The only proof of Honor is giving. Honor is the seed for protection and open windows. Tithe is a seed of honor." Dr. G*

| TOPIC | THOUGHT |
|-------|---------|

_____
_____
_____
_____
_____
_____
_____
_____
_____
_____
_____
_____
_____
_____
_____
_____
_____
_____
_____
_____
_____
_____
_____
_____

*"The most dangerous person in your life is the person who feeds your doubts."*
*Dr. G*

| TOPIC | THOUGHT |
|---|---|
|  |  |

| TOPIC | THOUGHT |
|-------|---------|

_"If you don't like your harvest, change your seed."_ Dr. G

| TOPIC | THOUGHT |
|---|---|

| TOPIC | THOUGHT |
|-------|---------|

_"If you want to stretch your living, stretch your thinking. Your mind is your world." Dr. G_

| TOPIC | THOUGHT |
|-------|---------|
|       |         |

| TOPIC | THOUGHT |
|-------|---------|

_____
_____
_____
_____
_____
_____
_____
_____
_____
_____
_____
_____
_____
_____
_____
_____
_____
_____
_____
_____
_____
_____
_____
_____
_____
_____
_____
_____
_____

*"Connection is any person God uses to link you to a desired change."* Dr. G

| TOPIC | THOUGHT |
|-------|---------|
|       |         |

| TOPIC | THOUGHT |
|-------|---------|

_____
_____
_____
_____
_____
_____
_____
_____
_____
_____
_____
_____
_____
_____
_____
_____
_____
_____
_____
_____
_____
_____
_____
_____
_____
_____

*"Never let your stuff create in you a greater feeling than your purpose! If you keep your purpose, you can always get your stuff back! Purpose always wins!"*
*Dr. G*

| TOPIC | THOUGHT |
|-------|---------|
|       |         |

| TOPIC | THOUGHT |
|-------|---------|

_____
_____
_____
_____
_____
_____
_____
_____
_____
_____
_____
_____
_____
_____
_____
_____
_____
_____
_____
_____
_____
_____
_____
_____
_____
_____
_____
_____
_____
_____

*"If God is for us, then it doesn't matter who is against us. If a man's way is pleasing to the Lord, He will make even His enemies to be at peace with him."*
*Dr. G*

| TOPIC | THOUGHT |
|-------|---------|

_"Be very focused on how you react to others. Remember, we are to be representing Kingdom love and not Kingdom justice! You may hurt God's witness." Dr. G_

TOPIC | THOUGHT

| TOPIC | THOUGHT |
|-------|---------|

_"Relationships work best when you're committed to the relationship and not just involved in it! Being for someone is greater than just doing for them!"_
_Dr. G_

| TOPIC | THOUGHT |
|-------|---------|

| TOPIC | THOUGHT |
|-------|---------|

_"The conquered have a different mindset than the conqueror! One complains about things; the other discusses plans to change things!" Dr. G_

| TOPIC | THOUGHT |
|-------|---------|
|       |         |

# FACTS ABOUT FAVOR

1. *Favor is when God causes someone to desire to become a problem solver in your life (Ruth 2:8-12).*
2. *Favor is a gift from God that can stop if it is not recognized and celebrated (Revelation 3:7).*
3. *Favor is only guaranteed to those who qualify through acts of obedience (Deuteronomy 28:1-2).*
4. *Success will require uncommon favor from someone (Deuteronomy 16:15).*
5. *Favor is an attitude of goodness toward you, not an exchange or payment for something you have done (Ruth 2:8-12).*
6. *Favor is an exception to the rule, not the normality (Psalm 127:1).*
7. *Favor must begin as a seed from you before it returns as a harvest to you (Galatians 6:7).*
8. *When you sow seeds of favor consistently, you will reap the harvest of favor consistently (Galatians 6:7-8).*
9. *The seed of favor can grow over a period of time (Luke 2:52).*
10. *Favor can make you wealthy in a single day (Ruth 4:13).*
11. *Favor can silence a lifetime enemy forever (Esther 3:5, 7:9-10).*
12. *Favor can make you a household name in 24 hours (Esther 2:16).*
13. *Favor can double your financial worth in the midst of your worst tragedy (Job 42:10-12).*
14. *Favor can accelerate the timetable of your assignment and destiny (Genesis 41:39-43).*
15. *One day of favor is worth a lifetime of labor (Ruth 4:10).*
16. *Favor comes when uncommon intercessors pray for you (Acts 12:5).*
17. *Favor always begins when you solve a problem for someone (Genesis 41:42-44).*

18. Currents of favor always flow when you solve the problem nearest you (Genesis 40:4-8).
19. Favor will usually come through someone observing you who is capable of greatly blessing you (Ruth 2:8-9).
20. Favor is not an accident, but a deliberate design by God to reward you for acts of obedience that are invisible to others (Isaiah 1:19).
21. Favor will stop when you deliberately ignore an instruction from God (I Samuel 15:-11, 26).
22. The flow of favor is often paralyzed through the self-development of arrogance and self-sufficiency (Daniel 5:20-21).
23. Favor can stop a tragedy instantly in your life (Genesis 41:39-40).
24. The river of favor will dry up when God observes greed (Malachi 3:8-9).
25. Favor is a seed that anyone can sow into the life of another (Ruth 2:8-9).
26. Favor should be pursued, requested and celebrated (Esther 5:1-4).
27. Favor is often the only exit from a place of captivity and bondage (Genesis 40:14).
28. Favor will cease when not received with thankfulness (Matthew 18:21-35).
29. Honoring your parents is the first clue to understanding the law of favor (Exodus 20:12).
30. Uncommon men always sow favor (Ruth 2:8-9).
31. The favor of God will always create favor with men (Luke 2:52).

# FACTS ABOUT THE HOLY SPIRIT

1. *The Holy Spirit is a person, not a dove, wind or fire (John 14:16).*
2. *The Holy Spirit created you (Job 33:4).*
3. *The Holy Spirit is the author of all scripture and the inspiration of all scripture (2 Timothy 3:16).*
4. *The Holy Spirit confirms that Jesus is within you (I John 4:13).*
5. *The Holy Spirit decides the skills, gifts and talents within you (I Corinthians 12:4-11).*
6. *The Holy Spirit gives life (2 Corinthians 3:6).*
7. *The Holy Spirit confirms you are a child of God (Romans 8:16).*
8. *The Holy Spirit imparts a personal prayer language that dramatically increases your strength and faith (Jude 1:20).*
9. *The Holy Spirit talks to you (Revelation 2:7).*
10. *The Holy Spirit reveals the truth you need to live victoriously (John 16:13).*
11. *The Holy Spirit is the Source of the Anointing…the special power of God given for your assignment (Luke 4:18).*
12. *The Holy Spirit is the Source of every desired emotion you are pursuing in your life (Galatians 5:22-23).*
13. *The Holy Spirit knows every detail of the purpose and plan of God for your life (Romans 8:27-28).*
14. *The Holy Spirit decides when you are ready to be tested (Luke 4:1-2).*
15. *The Holy Spirit is your intercessor on earth (Romans 8:26).*
16. *The Holy Spirit loves singing (Psalm 100:1-2).*
17. *The Holy Spirit is the source of your joy (Psalm 16:11).*
18. *The Holy Spirit is your only source of true peace (Galatians 5:22-23).*
19. *The Holy Spirit removes all fear (2 Timothy 1:7).*

20. The Holy Spirit shows you pictures of your future (John 16:13, Acts 7:55).
21. The Holy Spirit gives you the necessary love you need towards others (Romans 5:5).
22. The Holy Spirit decides your assignment (Acts 13:2-4).
23. The Holy Spirit enables you to enter into the Kingdom of God (John 3:5-6).
24. The Holy Spirit only guides those who are sons of God (Romans 8:14).
25. The Holy Spirit knows the person to whom you have been assigned (Acts 8:29).
26. The Holy Spirit will send inner warnings to protect you from wrong people and places (Acts 16:6-7).
27. The Holy Spirit is grieved and saddened by wrong conduct (Ephesians 4:30-31).
28. The Holy Spirit critiques every moment, motive and movement of your life (Jeremiah 17:10).
29. The Holy Spirit becomes an enemy to the rebellious (Isaiah 63:10).
30. The Holy Spirit withdraws when offended (Ephesians 4:30-32; Hosea 5:15).
31. The Holy Spirit raised Jesus from the dead, and He will raise you from the dead when Christ returns to the earth (Romans 8:11).

# FACTS ABOUT WISDOM

1. *Wisdom is the master key to all the treasures of life (2 Chronicles 1:7-8, 10-12; Colossians 2:2-3).*
2. *Wisdom is a gift from God to you (Proverbs 2:6; Daniel 2:21; I Corinthians 12:8).*
3. *The fear of God is the beginning of wisdom (Job 28:28; Psalm 111:10; Proverbs 9:10).*
4. *The wisdom of this world is a false substitute for the wisdom of God (I Corinthians 2:4, 13; James 3:13-17).*
5. *The wisdom of man is foolishness to God (I Corinthians 1:20-21, 25; 1 Corinthians 3:19).*
6. *Right relationships increase wisdom (Proverbs 13:20; I Corinthians 15:33; I Thessalonians 3:6; I Timothy 6:5).*
7. *The wisdom of God is foolishness to the natural mind (Proverbs 18:2; Isaiah 55:8-9; I Corinthians 2:4-5).*
8. *Your conversation reveals how much wisdom you possess (I Kings 10:24; Proverbs 18:21; Proverbs 29:11; James 3:2).*
9. *Jesus is made unto us wisdom (I Corinthians 1:30; Ephesians 1:5, 8, 17).*
10. *All the treasures of wisdom and knowledge are hidden in Jesus Christ (I Corinthians 1:23-24; I Corinthians 2:7-8; Colossians 2:2-3).*
11. *The word of God is your source of wisdom (Deuteronomy 4:5-6; Psalm 119:98-100; Proverbs 2:6).*
12. *God will give you wisdom when you take the time to listen (Proverbs 2:6; Isaiah 40:31; John 10:27; James 1:5).*
13. *The word of God is able to make you wise unto salvation (Psalm 107:43; John 5:39).*
14. *The Holy Spirit is the Spirit of wisdom that unleashes your gifts, talents and skills (Exodus 31:3-4; Exodus 36:1; Daniel 1:4).*

15. Men of wisdom will always be men of mercy (Galatians 6:1; James 3:17; James 5:19-20).
16. Wisdom is better than jewels or money (John 28:18; Proverbs 3:13-15; Proverbs 8:11; Proverbs 16:16).
17. Wisdom is more powerful than weapons of war (Proverbs 12:6; Ecclesiastes 9:18; Isaiah 33:6; Acts 6:10).
18. He that wins souls is wise (Proverbs 11:30; Daniel 12:3; Romans 10:14-15).
19. The wise hate evil and the evil hate the wise (Proverbs 1:7, 22; Proverbs 8:13; Proverbs 9:8; Proverbs 18:2).
20. Wisdom reveals the treasure in yourself (Proverbs 19:8; Ephesians 2:10; Philippians 1:6; I Peter 2:9-10).
21. The proof of wisdom is the presence of joy and peace (Psalm 119:165; Proverbs 3:13; Ecclesiastes 7:12; James 3:17).
22. Wisdom makes your enemies helpless against you (Proverbs 16:7; Ecclesiastes 7:12; Isaiah 54:17; Luke 21:15).
23. Wisdom creates currents of favor and recognition toward you (Proverbs 3:1-4; Proverbs 4:8; Proverbs 8:34-35).
24. The wise welcome correction (Proverbs 3:11-12; Proverbs 9:8-9)
25. When the wise speak, healing flows (Proverbs 10:11, 20, 21; Proverbs 12:18).
26. When you increase your wisdom you will increase your wealth (Psalm 112:1-3; Proverbs 3:16; Proverbs 8:18-21; Proverbs 14:24).
27. Wisdom can be imparted by the laying on of hands of a man of God (Deuteronomy 34:9; Acts 6:6-8, 10; 2 Timothy 1:6, 14).
28. Wisdom guarantees promotion (Proverbs 2:3-5; Proverbs 8:17, 21).
29. Wisdom loves those who love her (Proverbs 2:3-5; Proverbs 8:17, 21).

30. Wisdom will be given to you when you pray for it in faith (Matthew 7:7-8, 11; James 1:5-6).
31. The mantle of wisdom make you ten times stronger than those without it (Psalm 91:7; Ecclesiastes 7:19; Daniel 1:17, 20).

73488719R00089

Made in the USA
Columbia, SC
09 September 2019